# MOSSI

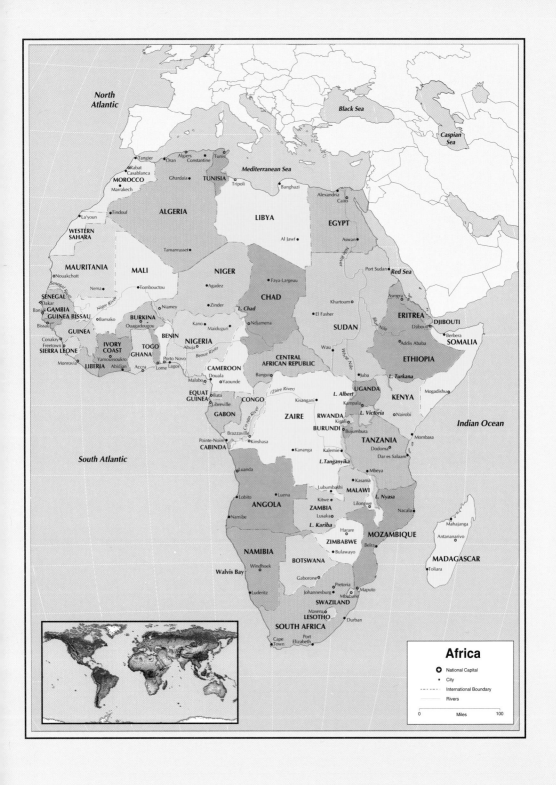

**North Atlantic**

**Black Sea**

**Caspian Sea**

Tangier
Rabat
Casablanca
**MOROCCO**
Marrakech

Algiers
Oran Constantine
Tunis
Ghardaïa
**TUNISIA**

**Mediterranean Sea**

Tripoli
Banghazi

Alexandria
Cairo

La'youn
Tindouf
**ALGERIA**

**LIBYA**

**EGYPT**

**WESTERN SAHARA**

Al Jawf
Aswan

Tamanrasset

Port Sudan
**Red Sea**

**MAURITANIA**
Nouakchott

**MALI**
Nema
Tombouctou

**NIGER**
Agadez

Zinder

**CHAD**
Faya-Largeau

Khartoum
**SUDAN**
El Fasher

Asmera
**ERITREA**
Djibouti
**DJIBOUTI**

Senegal R.
**SENEGAL**
Dakar
Banjul **GAMBIA**
**GUINEA BISSAU**
Bissau
**GUINEA**
Conakry
Freetown
**SIERRA LEONE**
Monrovia
**LIBERIA**

Bamako
Niger River
Niamey

Ouagadougou
**BURKINA**

**BENIN**

**NIGERIA**
Abuja

Kano Maiduguri
Ndjamena
L. Chad

Wau
**CENTRAL AFRICAN REPUBLIC**

Benue River

**IVORY COAST**
Yamoussoukro
Abidjan
**TOGO**
**GHANA**
Accra
Porto Novo
Lome Lagos

**CAMEROON**
Douala
Malabo
Yaounde
Bangui

Juba
White Nile
Blue Nile

Berbera
**SOMALIA**
Addis Ababa
**ETHIOPIA**
L. Turkana
Mogadishu

**EQUAT. GUINEA**
Bata
Libreville
**GABON**
**CONGO**

(Zaire River)
Kisangani
**ZAIRE**

L. Albert
**UGANDA**
Kampala
L. Victoria
**RWANDA**
Kigali
**BURUNDI**
Bujumbura

**KENYA**
Nairobi

Mombasa

**South Atlantic**

Pointe-Noire
Brazzaville
Kinshasa
**CABINDA**
Congo River

Kananga
Kalemie

**TANZANIA**
Dodoma
Dar es Salaam

**Indian Ocean**

Luanda

L.Tanganyika
Mbeya

Lobito
Luena
Lubumbashi
Kitwe
Kasama
**MALAWI**
L. Nyasa
Nacala

**ANGOLA**
Namibe

**ZAMBIA**
Lusaka
L. Kariba

Lilongwe

Harare
Belra
**MOZAMBIQUE**

Mahajanga
Antananarivo

**ZIMBABWE**
Bulawayo

**NAMIBIA**
Windhoek
**BOTSWANA**

**MADAGASCAR**
Toliara

**Walvis Bay**

Gaborone
Pretoria
Maputo

Luderitz
Johannesburg
Mbabane
**SWAZILAND**
Maseru
**LESOTHO**
Durban

**SOUTH AFRICA**
Cape Town
Port Elizabeth

## Africa

✪ National Capital
• City
‑ ‑ ‑ International Boundary
— Rivers

0     Miles     100

The Heritage Library of African Peoples

# MOSSI

Kibibi V. Mack-Williams, Ph.D.

THE ROSEN PUBLISHING GROUP, INC.
NEW YORK

Published in 1996 by The Rosen Publishing Group, Inc.
29 East 21st Street, New York, NY 10010

First Edition

Manufactured in the United States of America

**Library of Congress Cataloging-in-Publication Data**

Mack-Williams, Kibibi V., 1955–
    Mossi / Kibibi V. Mack-Williams. — 1st ed.
      p.  cm. — (The heritage library of African peoples)
    Includes bibliographical references and index.
    Summary: Describes the history, surroundings, politics, customs,
religion, and current situation of the Mossi people, who live in the
West African country of Burkina Faso.
    ISBN 0-8239-1984-6
    1. Mossi (African people)—History—Juvenile literature.  2. Mossi
(African people)—Social life and customs—Juvenile literature.
[1. Mossi (African people)]  I. Title.  II. Series.
DT555.45.M67M32  1995
966.25′004963—dc20                       95-20839
                                                 CIP
                                                 AC

# Contents

# INTRODUCTION

**THERE IS EVERY REASON FOR US TO KNOW** something about Africa and to understand its past and the way of life of its peoples. Africa is a rich continent that has for centuries provided the world with art, culture, labor, wealth, and natural resources. It has vast mineral deposits, fossil fuels, and commercial crops.

But perhaps most important is the fact that fossil evidence indicates that human beings originated in Africa. The earliest traces of human beings and their tools are almost two million years old. Their descendants have migrated throughout the world. To be human is to be of African descent.

The experiences of the peoples who stayed in Africa are as rich and as diverse as of those who established themselves elsewhere. This series of books describes their environment, their modes of subsistence, their relationships, and their customs and beliefs. The books present the variety of languages, histories, cultures, and religions that are to be found on the African continent. They demonstrate the historical linkages between African peoples and the way contemporary Africa has been affected by European colonial rule.

Africa is large, complex, and diverse. It encompasses an area of more than 11,700,000 square miles. The United States, Europe, and India could fit easily into it. The sheer size is an indication of the continent's great variety in geography, terrain, climate, flora, fauna, peoples, languages, and cultures.

Much of contemporary Africa has been shaped by European colonial rule, industrialization, urbanization, and the demands of a world economic system. For more than seventy years, large regions of Africa were ruled by Great Britain, France, Belgium, Portugal, and Spain. African peoples from various ethnic, linguistic, and cultural backgrounds were brought together to form colonial states.

For decades Africans struggled to gain their independence. It was not until after World War II that the colonial territories became independent African states. Today, almost all of Africa is ruled by Africans. Large numbers of Africans live in modern cities. Rural Africa is also being transformed, and yet its people still engage in many of their customs and beliefs.

Contemporary circumstances and natural events have not always been kind to ordinary Africans. Today, however, new popular social movements and technological innovations pose great promise for future development.

George C. Bond, Ph.D., Director
Institute of African Studies
Columbia University, New York

The majority of Mossi today still follow Mossi religion, particularly those in rural areas. About 40 percent of the population is Muslim and 10 percent is Christian. This Christian family lives in Ouagadougou, the capital of Burkina Faso.

chapter

# 1

# THE LAND

**MOST MOSSI PEOPLE TODAY LIVE IN BURKINA** Faso, a landlocked country in West Africa, where they make up about half of the total population.

Burkina Faso is north of Ghana and south of Mali and Niger. Burkina Faso's earlier name, Upper Volta, comes from the three rivers in the region: the Black, Red, and White Volta Rivers.

The south of Burkina Faso is wooded savanna; the north is semidesert. Most of the country consists of a vast plateau between 1,000 and 1,600 feet above sea level, dotted with low mountain ranges and numerous small hills. In the northeast, the Kipisi Mountains average 2,000 feet and include the sacred mountain of the Mossi, the Plimplikou. In the east lie the Boussouma Mountains, averaging 1,500 feet. Today, Mogho or "land of the Mossi" covers

Most Mossi live in Burkina Faso, formerly called Upper Volta.

some 30,000 square miles in the southern part of Burkina Faso.

Burkina Faso lies within the Sudanic climatic zone. It has mainly two seasons, one warm and dry and the other hot and wet. From November to mid-February the weather is dry and relatively cool, with an average temperature of 70 degrees. March to October is warmer and wetter; March and April have a short rainy season. The main rainy season, between June and October, has violent dust and rain storms and heavy showers and thunderstorms. The average temperature during the hot season is 88 degrees, and 75–80 in the warm season.

The rainy season is very important to the Mossi, who are a farming people. They cultivate millet, one of their staple foods, legumes, sorghum, maize, peanuts, onions, rice, beans, okra, yams, tobacco, cotton, and indigo. During dry periods crop production is low and can result in a food shortage leading to starvation and famine. The Sahara Desert is growing southward about four miles every year, so Burkina Faso is losing valuable farming land. Because of its climate and other factors, it is one of the world's poorest countries. Many Burkinabe (people from Burkina Faso) seek work in neighboring countries where climatic, economic, and living conditions are better.

The Mossi people are found in four major cities in Burkina Faso: Ouagadougou, Yatenga, Fada N'Gourma, and Tenkodogo. However, the vast majority of Mossi live in village-like, rural communities, with scattered neighborhoods ranging from five or six houses to as many as one hundred houses. Each neighborhood has a cluster of round, adobe houses built of dried mud bricks, with conical thatched roofs. Each house, or *yiri*, has its own courtyard, since the Mossi usually surround their homes with high mud or straw walls. Inside the courtyards, families raise sheep and goats.▲

Like most African peoples today, the Mossi continue to build traditional architecture in rural areas, but frequently this is blended with introduced building techniques and styles. Rural families live in a *yiri*, which has several structures and a courtyard enclosed by a high wall (top). Mud brick houses (middle) cost about $100 to build. Wealthy city dwellers, like the owner of this house (bottom), may spend a great deal more on a modern house in Western style.

# chapter

# 2
# THE PEOPLE

**THE MOSSI LIVE MAINLY BETWEEN THE RED** and White Volta Rivers in central Burkina Faso. The Mossi speak the More language. In addition to the Mossi, there are over sixty other ethnic groups in the country. For example, there are the Peul in the north, the Gurmantche and the Lela, Nuna, and Winiama in the west, the Lobi and Senufo in the southwest, and the Bobo and Dioula in the east. The Mossi are related to the Gurmantche and Yarse peoples.

Today, the Mossi divide themselves into occupational groups such as Saya (blacksmiths), Yarse (weavers), and Silmisi (herders).

The Mossi have a proud history because Mossi kingdoms were powerful in this region from about the 1300s until French colonization in the mid-1800s. Today many Mossi continue to respect their traditions regarding dress, reli-

A Mossi crowd, such as this one, reveals many different dress styles.
This woman wears rich jewelry and a hand-embroidered dress.

gion, work, and family and reject Westernization.
Although many Mossi speak French, they still
communicate in their language of More and
other regional languages such as Peul and Dioula.

For many Mossi men and women scarifica-
tion was an important sign of Mossi identity,
but it has now been forbidden by the government. A vertical line was cut from the temple to
the lower jaw, and a diagonal cut was made
from the bridge of the nose outward to the
cheek. Some women also scarified their breasts
and abdomen; others chose, instead, to have
their top front teeth filed to a point.

Mossi women often wear their hair in rows of
small braids. They often wear woven bands of
cotton cloth wrapped around the waist into a
skirt that reaches the middle of the calf. For
jewelry, they wear beautifully decorated rings,
anklets, and bracelets of copper and brass. They

either go barefoot or wear leather sandals. Mossi men usually wear loose-fitting, knee-length pants and sleeveless tunics made from woven strips of cotton. They often wear small round cotton caps. In the cities, Western dress or a mixture of African and Western clothing is worn.

The Mossi are renowned as expert craft workers. Blacksmiths make metal tools and jewelry of copper, zinc, and brass. They also carve

Mossi basketry.

wood to make mortars and pestles (used to grind grain), bowls, stools with legs in the shape of crocodiles or turtles, wooden doors, and sculpture. Women make many kinds of earthen pottery. Straw is used to make beautiful basketry and mats that are used for sitting and sleeping on as well as for doorway screens. The Mossi also weave and dye their own strips of cotton cloth, and they are famous as leather-

The Mossi have a reputation for fine crafts, which have always been important in their economy. Shown here are the weaving of long strips that are later sewn together (top), blacksmithing (middle), and pottery (bottom)

workers, making leather sandals, water pouches, and bags to hold grain, among other things.

### ▼ AGRICULTURE ▼

The land has always been very important in Mossi society. Before the introduction of Western ideas of ownership, the land was seen as a gift of God to all people, not to be owned by private individuals. It was property to be shared and used to help support each family and the entire community. It was the responsibility of Mossi chiefs to assign unoccupied land to people in need.

In the rural areas, women and children assist the men in farmwork. The men perform the heavier work such as the initial clearing of a field. Afterward, the women and children break up the clods, help fertilize the fields, collect dry brush for firewood, and assist the men in planting, cultivating, and harvesting crops. Millet grain is dried in the sun and then stored at home. Dried millet stalks are used for firewood.

At the end of their harvest season, the Mossi give a portion of their crops or produce to their ruler, the Mogho Naba, during a big harvest ceremony called the Soretasgho. During the festivities, the wives in the royal household of the Mogho Naba prepare refreshments to serve to the guests and village people attending the ceremony. The Mossi are well known for their many elaborate ceremonies.

At the Soretasgho harvest festival, the Mossi present a portion of their crops to
their chief. Here the gifts are laid out in the courtyard of the chief of Sapone.

The Mossi have many elaborate ceremonies, such as this one for the chief's festival called Na Poosum.

Mossi diet includes goat and sheep meat, fish, millet, yams, and milk. Beef is not usually eaten, since they raise cattle mostly for milk and for export. However, cows that are too old for milking or export are eaten. Donkeys are used for work and transportation.

### ▼ DOMESTIC SLAVERY ▼

In the ancient past, the Mossi practiced a form of slavery called domestic slavery. This differed from the chattel slavery practiced later in the Americas. Domestic slaves were not purchased to work to earn money for their masters like chattel slaves, nor were they treated cruelly. They were not normally sold, and families were not separated. Slaves were sold only if they became convicted criminals. However, the Mossi were also known for castrating some slaves to provide eunuchs for sale to the trans-Saharan caravan traders.

The Mossi slave system resembled a kinship system that served to increase its own population, with the slaves themselves being eventually treated as members of the slave-owner's extended family. Slaves were usually war captives or their descendants. They gradually became assimilated into Mossi society and eventually accepted the village where they lived as their new home and the Mossi as their new family. Slaves performed the same tasks as the free Mossi. They did repairs, provided firewood, fed the livestock, and cultivated the fields, usually alongside the family. Slaves were used in the palace of the Mogho Naba to serve the family and guests, cultivate crops, and care for the animals.

### ▼ TRADERS ▼

Mossi traders in the past were usually men. However, both men and women provided the goods for the long-distance trade from West Africa across the Sahara Desert.

At the height of the Saharan trade, which lasted until the end of the 1500s, Mossi men traveled to Timbuktu in Mali to trade their goods at the great market there. They traded lead, iron, antimony, strips of woven cotton, leatherwork, straw hats, pots, jars, calabashes, rice, peppers, kola nuts, tobacco, dried fish and onions, peanuts, millet, mats, and soap. They returned with such wares as needles, mirrors, carpets, fezzes, salt, coffee, tea, beads, perfumes, and robes to sell at their local markets.

Today, Burkina Faso's most important trade routes are to ports in Côte d'Ivoire and Togo. Their major export is cattle, but all imports and exports follow these routes by train, truck, and on foot. Forty percent of imports come from France, and Burkina has much debt. The decline of the trans-Sahara trade and start of European influence contributed to the change of fortune in this part of Africa. Furthermore, desertification, soil deterioration, and population increases have made agricultural production insufficient. This has forced the Burkinabe to become migrant laborers in neighboring countries or in the food factories and industries in Ouagadougou.

Today there are thus fewer people to grow food in Mossi villages. Women, children, and old men attempt to grow the food they need, but to support themselves they are usually forced to work on French-owned plantations growing commercial crops. Much of the money earned in this way is used to buy foods that the Mossi once produced themselves.

Today many Mossi are migrant laborers. Many Mossi work in the factories around the capital city of Ouagadougou. This is the brick factory on the north side of the city.

Some Mossi today are concerned about the possibility of the migrants losing their Mossi identity as a result of settling in other countries. They discourage marriages of Mossi men to foreign women who will raise the children to identify with her culture. A child raised by a non-Mossi mother is no longer regarded as a Mossi.

Mossi women scarcely participate openly in Mossi politics; however, they belong to a women's society led by the *magajia*, an elderly woman. This organization addresses some of the needs and problems of women. It collects money for women who have given birth to a child, who are getting married, or who need to bury someone who has died. It also contributes to the various ceremonies held throughout the year. Today many Mossi women are very active in trade and spend a significant part of their day at the market.

### ▼ THE FAMILY ▼

The Mossi believe that their physical and spiritual qualities come from both their mother and father. The Mossi mother is largely responsible for the children's developing a strong love for and identity with Mossi culture.

Polygamy is common among the Mossi. A wealthy man can have more than one wife if he can afford to take care of them. The joint wives usually live together peacefully. The husband provides each with her own house inside the walled or fenced compound. In the shared courtyard children play while women make crafts, prepare food, and cook millet cakes and porridges that are served with a variety of vegetable and meat sauces.

Aside from raising their own children, Mossi women also look after their co-wives' children and help each other prepare food for the family and visitors. If their husband's elderly mother lives in the household, they take turns cleaning her house and preparing her meals.

When little boys are old enough to feed themselves, they are sent to eat with their fathers and elderly male relatives. In this way they learn the culture of the Mossi men. The little boys run errands for the men and observe them repairing tools, herding the animals, or working in the millet fields. By the age of twelve, Mossi boys have become good farmers.

Mossi girls stay around their mother or female relatives. They begin to help with the cooking before they are seven. They gather firewood, hunt wild plants for dinner, fetch water from the well, and care for their younger siblings. They are also taught how to spin cotton into thread. By age eight, they are taken to the fields to be taught farmwork.

A Mossi girl may marry at thirteen, to a man in his mid- or late twenties. If she is his first wife, he does not marry another woman until he reaches his thirties and is wealthier. A Mossi bride usually stays with her husband's father at first. This is like a training period during which she does much of the housework for her father-in-law's wives. If her husband is already married, the young bride moves into her new home and is expected to do most of the housework for her co-wives. In either case, before marriage she is trained by her mother and given various cooking utensils and new clothes to start her off in her married lifestyle. ▲

# chapter

# 3

# THE MOSSI KINGDOMS

THE MOSSI PEOPLE TRACE THEIR ORIGINS BACK to Naba Nedega of Gambaga. He invaded from east of Lake Chad and conquered the peoples living between the Red and White Volta Rivers in the 11th century. The invaders dominated the entire region of present-day northern Ghana and southeast Burkina Faso by the 14th century and intermarried with the indigenous people.

According to Mossi oral history, Naba Nedega was much attached to his daughter, Nyennega, who was also a great warrior, and he did not want her to marry. She fell in love with a Mande hunter called Riale and ran away to marry him. She named her first son after the horse that took her away, Ouedraogo, which means "stallion."

When Ouedraogo was older, Nyennega sent him to Gambaga to visit her father, who welcomed him immediately. Ouedraogo told him of Nyennega's unhappy marriage and request for help. Naba Nedega sent her horses, cows, and warriors. Later, Ouedraogo and his troops conquered her village of Tankourou, settled there, and intermarried with its women. According to legend, this assimilation of peoples and cultures formed the Mossi people. As more and more people migrated to the village, intermarried, and had children, the Mossi population increased.

### ▼ EXPANSION ▼

Ouedraogo conquered the smaller villages nearby and expanded his kingdom, called Tenkodogo. After Ouedraogo's death, his son defeated their most powerful enemy, the Wogodogo kingdom. With this victory, Wogodogo and its capital became the center of Mossi power. The population increased immensely as surrounding villages were absorbed. Many Muslim refugees fleeing their warring villages and Muslim merchants seeking trade relations settled there, contributed to its growth and wealth, and introduced Muslim cultural influence.

There were six important Mossi kingdoms: Tenkodogo, Wogodogo, Yatenga, Fada N'Gurma, Kaya, and Bulsa. Fada N'Gurma, the center of the Gurmantche people's territory, was the first kingdom. Later, one of Ouedraogo's descen-

dants broke away from Wogodogo and formed
the rival kingdom of Yatenga. With its capital
at Ouahigouya, Yatenga was strong by the
1700s.

These Mossi kingdoms all had strong capitals
ruled by kings who controlled trade. The region's great trading empires of Mali (powerful in
the 1200s and 1300s) and Songhay (1400s and
1500s) were important trading partners and
rivals of the Mossi kingdoms. Mali and Songhay
were too strong to conquer, but the Mossi frequently raided them.

The Mossi were proud of their cavalry and
the fighting skills that enabled them to defeat
others, expand their kingdoms, and protect their
own kingdoms from invasion. One of their most
famous wars was fought in 1483 when the
Mossi invaded the powerful kingdom of
Songhay, then ruled by Sonni Ali. For the next
century, Songhay and Mossi attacked each other
sporadically, but in the end, the superior
Songhay army defeated the Mossi.

The Mossi army carried rawhide shields and
was armed with bows and arrows, spears,
swords, and clubs. Warriors used short arrows,
their iron tips coated with poison that paralyzed
the heart. Some warriors carried guns purchased
from the trade caravans. Such weapons made
them invincible to nearby armies. Furthermore,
the Mossi army was spiritually inspired. Warriors
wore amulets around their necks or arms, which

they believed protected them from harm.

The Mossi usually sent scouts ahead to spy on the enemy. Scouts were camouflaged with leaves and branches and crawled on the ground.

Most wars were fought during the dry season. The planting season required both male and female labor; thus the Mossi could not afford a powerful standing army.

In warfare, the Mossi generally burned the enemy's village, took its livestock, and sold its youth into domestic slavery. If defeated, they usually abandoned their dead and dying soldiers. When victorious, however, they carried their dead and wounded back home for proper burial or medical care. When a Mossi kingdom was attacked, the people immediately evacuated the village or barricaded it with trees, trenches, and poisoned foot traps.

### ▼ THE COMING OF ISLAM ▼

The Mossi's contact with outside people was largely limited to other African ethnic groups and Muslim Arab traders and refugees. Muslims first came to Mossi territories in the late 1490s and attempted to convert the Mogho Naba in Ouagadougou and his subjects, first by persuasion and then by Muslim holy war or *jihad*. They failed. Later Muslim refugees, fleeing wars in West Africa, came to settle and did not try to spread Islam.

Horses are important in Mossi history and helped the Mossi conquer others. Muslim immigrants contributed to the growth of trading centers. Here a Muslim rider stops to pray, facing in the direction of Mecca, the holy city of Muslims.

At first Mossi rulers restricted Muslims to living and worshiping in certain places, but later these restrictions were lifted. With time, a few Mossi rulers converted to Islam. By the mid-1700s, Islam had spread gradually into many Mossi districts. The Naba allowed the Muslims to have an Imam, or priest, as their representative in the government. The Imam wore a white turban and a white robe presented to him by the Naba. He gave praise to his God, Allah, and paid tribute to Nabiyama, the Mossi name for the prophet Muhammad, who founded Islam in 622 AD. Most Mossi rulers eventually had Muslims among their councillors. Widely traveled and exposed to foreign cultures and people, they were able to give advice to the Naba when foreign visitors arrived in Mossi kingdoms.▲

# chapter

# 4

# POLITICAL LIFE AND CUSTOMS

## ▼ BEFORE COLONIZATION ▼

Before European colonization in the 1800s, the Mossi kingdoms had a highly organized political system.

Today, as in the past, Mossi kings and chiefs hold title through descent traceable back to the time of Naba Nedega's invasion. The invaders became the ruling class, called the Nakomse ("rulers"). They ruled over the people they conquered, known as the Tengabisi or Nyonyose ("the old ones"). The title of the Mossi king was Naba, Na, or Nab. The leaders of principalities or states were called Dim; those of districts, Kombemba; and those of villages, Tense Nanamse. The Mossi insisted that the relationship between the Naba and the Dim be similar to that of a father and elder son. Hence, the Dim was able to run his own village and make

Mossi chiefs have authority over many decisions. This chief, in blue, makes a decision on behalf of the man who sits in a pose of respect beside his harvest.

major decisions without conferring with the Naba each time.

The Naba and the Dim usually appointed their sons or younger brothers to be Kombemba. These familial appointments kept the ruling power within the royal lineage. A chief was an honored man of nobility in his district. Nobles were allowed to marry more wives than other men and thus could have more children. This added to their high status in society.

Four Mossi kingdoms had individual kings. The Mogho Naba of Ouagadougou was a more powerful king than the Yatenga Naba, the Tenkodogo Naba and the Fada N'Gourma Naba. He became the preeminent Mossi ruler and set the general pattern of chieftainship in Mossi territory. The Mogho Naba maintained grand pomp and ceremony in his court, which was imitated on a much smaller scale by the other Nabas. It was forbidden to touch his hand or to speak to him without kneeling with one's forehead on the ground. People were expected to hesitate before pronouncing his name, and no one else was allowed to have his name.

From the colonial period onward the power of Mossi kings and nobles declined. However, it was only in 1984 that the tribute labor and taxes that Mossi rulers received from their subjects were abolished. Mossi nobles still have considerable local power in modern Burkina Faso.

## ▼ THE ROYAL FAMILY ▼

In precolonial Mossi society, the average woman was not overtly involved in political activity; her status was usually dependent on that of her husband. Only the wives of the Mossi king played a significant political role. The most active woman at the court of the Naba was the Pughtiema, the Naba's first wife or head wife. She was the only wife he introduced to his friends and whom his subjects were allowed to visit. The Pughtiema served as the official hostess at certain ceremonies, and it was her task to prepare the special millet beer and millet water for ceremonial offering to the ancestors. She was usually older than the other wives, generally past childbearing age, and was responsible for handling any problems between other wives.

The other royal wives were divided into three groups. The first group were the *zaka sanga*, or large courtyard. These women lived with the Pughtiema and were also past childbearing age. They had their own fields to cultivate with the help of their children and servant page boys.

The second group were the *zagbilin*, or small courtyard. These women, mostly in their thirties and forties, also had their own fields to cultivate with the help of select young men from the court. The *zagbilin* who were relatively young and still raising children continued to receive occasional visits from the Naba.

The last group of wives were the *dogunba*, the keepers of the household. This was the most important group. They prepared the Naba's meals and spent much of their time with him. They were young and fertile. The *dogunba* generally were better dressed and received the most attention from the Naba. They, like the *zaka sanga* and the *zagbilin*, also cultivated their own fields.

## ▼ THE NABA ▼

The Naba was held in the highest esteem. It was believed that the Mossi people could not live properly without their ruler. They looked to the Naba to set administrative policy and deal with other important issues. If an outsider visited one of the kingdoms, he was brought before

the Naba. The Naba was expected to keep the
peace within his kingdom at all times, even
when the Mossi were at war with another state.
He was expected to be fair and impartial when
making decisions. The Naba was responsible for
assuring that the ancestors brought health and
prosperity to the people. Thus, it was imperative
that the Naba supervise and participate in all
ceremonies pertaining to the ancestors.

When the Naba died, the Mossi were not
notified until the crown prince had arrived. The
people mourned the Naba's death in an elaborate ceremony. Libations were offered to the
ancient rulers. The heads of all important officials and royal family members were shaved to
signify they were in mourning. On the eighth
day after the Naba's death, the actual funeral
ceremony took place. It included several ceremonial animal sacrifices to the ancestors of the
Naba.

In precolonial Mossi society, there were no
written laws. Instead, minor problems were usually resolved between the conflicting parties.
Serious problems were handled by judges or
chiefs. Punishment for crimes included flogging,
banishment from the village, or execution. Today
Mossi customary law exists alongside the judicial
system introduced by the French and extended
by Burkinabe legislators.

Burkina Faso is now ruled by a president, not

The Burkina Faso army in an Independence Day parade on the grand avenue of Ouagadougou.

a Mossi chief. Yet the country still pays homage to its chiefs by honoring them on Independence Day. A law passed in 1962 states that only the Mossi chiefs are allowed to wear their traditional robes and headdresses. The chiefs also receive a yearly stipend to help them live.▲

# chapter

# 5
# RELIGION

**PRECOLONIAL MOSSI RELIGION CENTERED**
around their ancestors and the earth. The Mossi
believed that all things on the land belonged to
the earth deity, Tenga Wende. Therefore, any
item of importance or value that was found
should be taken to the earth shrine, which was
usually a large tree. There, the Mossi believed,
either the proper owner would come to claim
the lost article or eventually the article would
decompose and return to the earth.

The Tengsobadamba, or priests, were the
custodians of the holy earth shrines. Their
spiritual leadership in society was as significant
as that of the Naba. Politics was the realm of
the rulers, the invading horsemen from the
south. Religion was the realm of the conquered
farmers. It was not unusual for the ruler to
perform certain religious ceremonies. Since all

the Mossi rulers descended from Nyennega of Dagomba, they were ancestral kin. This kinship provided them with a spiritual link that allowed them to have special roles in religious ceremonies.

The Mossi calendar is divided into twelve moons, each of which had a ceremony associated with it. The Mossi celebrated the same ceremonies but at different times, because the climate and farming activity vary throughout Mossi country. For example, although the moon during the rainy season calls for a certain ceremony, it will not take place in areas where the rainy season has not yet started. Ceremonies were also sometimes called by different names.

### ▼ CEREMONIES ▼

Of the several religious ceremonies held in the Mossi kingdoms, the largest was and still is held in Ouagadougou, which has the largest population. A New Year's ceremony, Sigim-Dam, is held throughout Mossi society at varying times in January, depending on when the first moon of the Mossi year appears. This traditional ceremony gives thanks to the earth deity for good crops during the past year and thanks in advance for heavy rains that will provide another good crop.

The festival marks the beginning of the farming season. It is held at mid-morning. All the

Religion and politics are closely related for most Mossi. Celebrations for the Ombila chiefs, such as this one, are spiritual occasions.

religious leaders and important officials of the city are clad in special ceremonial clothing and arrive at the palace very early. The Naba is saluted and wished a prosperous new year for himself and his subjects. In turn, the Naba presents gifts to the religious leaders and officials and provides much food and drink. The musicians beat their drums all day and sing praises to both their ruler and the ancestors. The musicians also receive gifts from the Naba, such as long robes made of beautiful material. Similar ceremonies are held throughout Mossi country.

Another major traditional ceremony places the earth deity, Tenga Wende, at the center of the celebration. It focuses on celebrating the productivity of the land and the importance of royal ancestors. This ceremony played a major role in uniting the Mossi people throughout the kingdoms. It celebrated both the earth deity of the Tengabisi and the royal line of the Nakomse conquerers. It also strengthened the bond between the Naba and the lesser chiefs and elders. Many people came together to eat and enjoy the food they had worked so hard to produce from the land.

This ceremony was also a fertility rite and a festival in honor of female ancestors. It was normally held before the crops were sowed. Animal sacrifices were made over the graves of the former rulers before the actual ceremony began. Once the Naba had met with the Larhalle Naba, the local religious leader, the celebration was scheduled to begin throughout Mossi territory within twenty-one days.

The Larhalle Naba then made five cords out of tree bark and tied 19 knots in each one. He passed these cords on to each provincial minister in the five provinces. Each day, the ministers untied one knot to indicate that another day had passed and to remind them of how many days were left before the ceremony began.

When only one knot was left on the cords, messengers carried the cords throughout the kingdoms to announce that the festival would soon begin. The cords were then returned to the ministers. On the Friday morning before the ceremony, the Larhalle Naba knelt before the Naba and untied the last knot, signifying that the ceremony would start the next day. The

At the chief's festival, Na Poosum, "Greet the Chief," the chief's family gather around the royal tombs on which are placed wooden figures of the chief's ancestors. Here figures belonging to the chief La Titon stand on the ancestral grave shrine in front of the palace entrance.

Naba then gave bars of salt to members of the royal court and his visitors.

Early on Saturday morning, royal servants brought huge quantities of food, including beef and mutton cooked without pepper, a spice disliked by the ancestors, and huge pots of millet beer. Once the ceremony began, the Larhalle Naba entered wearing a new white robe given him by the Naba. He then took three portions of the stiff millet porridge, dipped it in a special sauce, and threw the porridge in three directions to the waiting ancestral spirits.

The Larhalle Naba then called for the royal spirits, the deceased ministers' spirits, and the ancestral spirits to grant a long life to the Naba and peace to all the Mossi people. He repeated the blessing using morsels of meat and portions of millet beer. Afterward, the Gande Naba, the Mossi holy man participating in the ritual, picked up the food thrown to the ancestors and carried it away. In doing this, he never looked back, fearing that seeing the ancestors would result in death. Once the Gande Naba was gone, the actual festivities began as the people rushed forward to enjoy the food and drink.

Throughout the kingdoms, the festivities lasted only a few days. In the large kingdom of Ouagadougou, however, it lasted almost four weeks. Near the end, the Larhalle Naba returned all cords to the Naba. Once the final sacrifices of white roosters had been made, the feathers and blood were placed on the axes used to kill the animals in the ceremony. The Mossi believed that this increased the power of the ceremonial axes. Mutton, millet cakes, and other gifts were then presented to select royal kin to conclude the celebration.

### ▼ SACRIFICES ▼

It was common for the Naba to offer sacrifices throughout the year to prevent such evils as drought, famine, flooding, epidemics, and, later, the influx of French colonials into Mossi land. At times, the Naba called for the district and village chiefs to perform similar sacrifices to the earth shrines by sacrificing animals and pouring drinks of millet beer and millet water.

The Mossi rulers who became Muslims continued to revere their ancestors, but they also participated in important Muslim festivals. For example, at the Muslim feast of Tabaski in honor of Muslim religious leaders the Naba would send the Imam cattle and sheep to be sacrificed. He joined the Imam and others in prayer and allowed the sacrificial ceremony to be held in the palace. The Naba himself held the tail of the animal while the Imam performed the ritual. Afterward, the Naba provided the Muslims with millet water and food.

Mossi who are not Muslim also participate in

the big festival that ends the month-long fast of Ramadan observed by Muslims. Although the early Mossi rulers and the people did not participate in the fast, they supported the holiday. When the crescent moon appeared in the sky, marking the end of Ramadan, the Mossi fired shots into the sky and launched arrows to celebrate.

The Naba attended the prayer service at the mosque with the Muslims the next morning and presented the Imam with gifts. In return, the Imam also showered the Naba with gifts. The Muslims were then served millet water sweetened with honey, millet cakes, meat, and kola nuts. The Mossi people and the Muslims continued to have a strong, peaceful relationship throughout the period of the Mossi kingdoms' power, from around the 1400s until the beginning of European colonization.

Today the Mossi follow their traditional religion, Islam, Christianity, or a mixture of these belief systems. While estimates vary, some believe that at least 75 percent of Mossi follow traditional religion today. This percentage may be as high as 90 percent in rural areas, although traditional religion there is often blended with Muslim practices. The high estimates for Muslim and Christian followers among the Mossi are 40 percent and 10 percent respectively. Generally, the north of Burkina Faso is more

Muslim. Cities contain a higher proportion of Christian and Muslim followers than rural areas.

## ▼ ART ▼

Art is an important part of Mossi religion. Wooden masks and figures are used to worship the ancestors and earth deities that control the weather and human fortunes. These sculptures are regarded as living beings that play a vital role in Mossi religion. Through prayers and offerings to these beings, the Mossi ask their ancestors and the earth spirits to ensure a good harvest and a healthy life.

Unlike sacred art in other cultures, Mossi masks and especially the statues are hidden and rarely seen. The masks emerge from the bush during initiations and funerals. While masks are owned and used only by the Tengabisi clans, statues are owned and used only by the ruling Nakomse clans. Masks are named after Tengabisi spirits, while statues are named after deceased rulers. These masks and figures are living links between the ancestors and their descendants. They affirm the power of the ruling lineages and the forces of the spirit world.

The Mossi word for mask is *Wango*. Each clan has a totem animal represented by a mask. For example, there is *wan-silga* the hawk mask, *wan-pesego* the ram mask, and *wan-nyaka* the small antelope, to name a few. The Mossi use these

These impressive masks appeared at important funerals, such as this one of the head of the Sawadogo clan from the village of Samba, north of Yako.

At the New Year festival, Sigim-Dam, village ancestors are honored and asked for their blessings for the coming year. Here a male mask dances in the village of Zeguedeguin.

masks to escort the body of the deceased to the grave. The masks are regarded as living forms of the ancestors, strange beings speaking in a secret whistling language. They are an awesome sight as they emerge from the dry bush and enter the village to visit the living. They serve as an honor guard. Brandishing whips and sticks, with which they sometimes attack the villagers, they make

Masks perform at Mossi funerals, like this one in Sini, in the eastern Mossi area. The large mask is a male mask that honors the spirits of nature. The dwarf bush spirit masks watch.

sure that the burial ceremonies are properly performed. Several months after the burial, the masks reappear. After receiving sacrifices of millet beer and chicken, they escort the spirit of the deceased to the spirit world.

In a spectacular annual drama at the beginning of the rainy season, all the masks come together for the Sigim-Dam ceremony. During this time, all the clans in every village gather to make sacrifices, to drink, and to offer the masks large quantities of millet beer. In continuing to honor the earth spirits and ancestors in their traditional ways, the Mossi continue an ancient and vital tradition.▲

# chapter

# 6

# COLONIZATION AND INDEPENDENCE

## ▼ EARLY CONTACT ▼

Early European contact with Africa occurred mostly along the coast of Africa. The European traders did not often venture into the interior because of rumors of unfriendly people, deadly disease, or myths of cannibalism or monsters. Still, they did hear about the magnificent trading centers in the Mossi kingdoms somewhere in the interior of West Africa.

The Portuguese were the first Europeans to hear about the Mossi people in the late 1400s but failed to make contact with them. It was not until the 1800s that they again become interested in finding the Mossi kingdoms to establish trade relations. However, the Ashanti, the Hausa, and other African traders living in the coastal cities prevented the Portuguese and other

48

Europeans from entering the interior and finding their trade sources.

After the British defeated the Ashanti in the late 1800s, they and French, Portuguese, and other European explorers and traders entered the African interior in search of gold, ivory, and other goods. After a while, the European groups began to argue with each other over who held the trade rights on certain goods. They agreed to settle their differences in a series of meetings known as the Berlin Conference, held in Germany in 1884–1885. Their major resolution was to divide up the African continent so that each European country would control its own area to explore and exploit without interference from the others.

Great Britain and France already had experience in setting up and ruling colonies in Asia and the Americas. (In fact, both the English and the French had experienced a rebel colony gaining its independence—the United States and Haiti respectively.) As a result of their experience, they had well-developed policies that they believed should be practiced in Africa. The British adopted indirect rule, by which they determined the policies used in each colony but they hand-picked African chiefs to implement the policies. In contrast, the French adopted a policy of direct rule and assimilation, under which Africans could in theory become assimi-

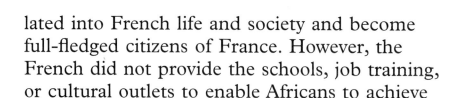

lated into French life and society and become full-fledged citizens of France. However, the French did not provide the schools, job training, or cultural outlets to enable Africans to achieve such assimilation.

Politically, the French divided their African colonies into two large blocs called French West Africa and French Equatorial Africa. Each bloc of colonies had a French governor-general and a council, and each individual colony had a French lieutenant governor and an advisory council.

In 1886 a German trader entered Ouagadougou to stay for several months, while traveling with a trading caravan. The Mossi kingdoms were losing their isolation from European contact and exploitation. Eventually, the Germans, French, and English all competed for control of the Mossi kingdoms, knowing that whoever owned the Mossi markets would also control all the commercial trade in the interior around the Niger River.

By 1890, the French sent a representative to meet with the Mogho Naba of Ouagadougou to convince him that the Europeans wanted only friendship. However, the Mogho Naba, the majority of the Mossi people, and the kingdom's small Muslim community did not trust the French. They believed strongly that if one European came, others would follow until they were numerous enough to control the Mossi people.

The Muslims were particularly influential in helping to slow the entrance of Europeans into the Mossi kingdoms. They counseled the Mossi rulers and warned them of the Europeans' intentions. While the Mossi were suspicious of the Europeans and opposed to a large European presence in the kingdoms, they did agree to establish trade relations with the French.

## ▼ FRENCH RULE ▼

The French were at war with Ahmadu, the ruler of the land north of Mossi country, and defeated his army in 1893. Later, the French commander sent a message to the Mogho Naba of Ouagadougou, requesting that he sign a treaty with the French. The Mogho Naba refused and sent a message instructing the French to stay away, since the Mossi did not want to fall under French rule. Nevertheless, in 1896 the Mossi kingdoms were invaded and defeated by the French. The Naba of Ouagadougou took refuge in Dagomba, a city south of Ouagadougou.

The French policy of direct rule met with strong resistance from the Mossi people, causing the French to adopt a more decentralized, indirect rule. As in the British colonies, the practice of hand-picking the chiefs was the only way the early French could control the Mossi. For example, the leadership of Saidou Congo, a member of the traditional Mossi dynasty, was opposed by the Mossi electoral council because of his youth and immaturity. The French nevertheless secured his election through bribes, believing that they could easily control him. Through such puppets, all major policies regarding taxation, the military, and the labor force were controlled by the French.

Under French rule, the Mossi kingdoms were first called the Upper Ivory Coast and then the Upper Volta. In 1919 Upper Volta was finally constituted as a territory after more than twenty years of resistance to French rule. The revolts of 1919 were mercilessly suppressed, and tens of thousands of people were deported to neighboring countries to work in plantations and mines and were forced to build roads and ports. In 1932 the territory of Upper Volta was dismantled and divided between Côte d'Ivoire, Niger, and French Sudan. Upper Volta's borders were finalized only in 1947.

The French eliminated the Mossi political system and set up a French government using a hand-picked ruler, the Naba. Under this system, the Naba had little or no power. Having divided up the Mossi country, the French appointed new leaders who they knew would cooperate with them. Such leaders commonly accepted bribes and were easily controlled. Mossi people who refused to cooperate were arrested or ex-

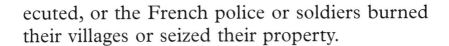

ecuted, or the French police or soldiers burned their villages or seized their property.

### ▼ TAXATION SYSTEM ▼

The French required the Mossi to pay taxes to support the colonial government. The Mossi people did use French currency, but had no French money. They were forced to change their lifestyle. They not only performed their traditional jobs of trading, farming, hunting, and raising their families, but had to earn French money by working for the benefit of the colonial state. The French-appointed chiefs were given the responsibility of recruiting the Mossi for work.

Men constructed buildings, roads, bridges, and telegraph poles and extracted natural resources from the earth; women and men participated in planting crops, all to be sold by the French to other countries. If any people refused to work or pay taxes, their property was confiscated and sold, or they were arrested and punished.

The Mossi were paid very little for their work. Many of the jobs were very dangerous, and large numbers of Mossi men died. Because of this, the Mossi people resisted the chiefs' attempts to recruit them for work.

Under French colonial rule, a few sons of chiefs were educated and learned French in or-

der to work in low-level government jobs. Mossi
women and girls were neither educated nor
hired to work. However, as the French mission-
aries established more churches and missionary
schools, girls and boys other than the chiefs'
sons were educated.

### ▼ POLITICAL ACTION ▼

After World War II, Africans in French colonies became very active politically and formed
their own organizations. The Mossi and other
African ethnic groups living in Upper Volta
formed two main parties. The Union Voltaique
was controlled largely by the Mogho Naba of
Ouagadougou, Sagha IV. One of its members,
Maurice Yameogo, became one of the country's
leading statesmen. The other party, the Ras-
semblement Democratique Africain (RDA), was
active throughout colonial French West Africa.
Ouezzin Coulibaly from Upper Volta emerged
as one of the main leaders of the RDA. The
Union Voltaique was later called the Mouve-
ment Democratique Voltaique (MDV), and the
RDA was renamed the Union Democratique
Voltaique or the UDV-RDA.

By 1949, these political parties came together
to form a General Council. Since the majority of
people in Upper Volta belonged to the Mossi
ethnic group, they held the most political seats.

In 1952, the Mossi chiefs formed the Union

of the Traditional Chiefs of Upper Volta. The organization assisted poor women, children, and other Mossi people in need. Eventually the Union united with traditional chiefs from other countries in French-ruled West Africa to oppose the minor roles that the French gave them in the colonial government. A younger, educated group of Mossi men, usually called the "educated elite," challenged both the French-appointed chiefs and colonial rule. They demanded self-rule for the Mossi and other Africans.

In a referendum in 1958, French President Charles de Gaulle offered the colonies in West Africa the choice of being totally independent or becoming part of a Franco-African community. The colony of Guinea was the only one to vote for a complete break with the French colonial empire. However, once Guinea became independent, the French retaliated by suspending all financial aid, technical assistance, and investment in industry. The French also destroyed military equipment and archival materials. Guinea was devastated but sought assistance from other European countries.

Upper Volta, on the other hand, voted to become part of the Franco-African community. When Ouezzin Coulibaly of the UDV-RDA died in 1958, Maurice Yameogo became the new leader, even though he had opposed the RDA in the past. The UDV-RDA party won 64 out of 75 seats in the elections held in 1959. Thereafter Upper Volta united with Côte d'Ivoire, Benin, and Niger to form the Council of the Entente. After much discussion, debate, and compromise, Upper Volta gained its independence from France on August 5, 1960.

The first President was Maurice Yameogo, leader of the UDV, which was an extension of the RDA led by Felix Houphuet Boigny, first President of Côte d'Ivoire.

### ▼ AFTER INDEPENDENCE ▼

Since independence in 1960 there have been several governments controlled by the military. In 1966, after six years of increasingly harsh and corrupt government, the army overthrew Yameogo, created a military council, and installed president Sangoule Lamizana. In 1975, after a general strike, a new government was formed. In 1978, Joseph Ouedraogo of the UDV-RDA won an election and assembled another government. There was yet another general strike in 1980 and another military coup, this time led by Colonel Saye Zerbo. In 1982, Saye Zerbo was overthrown by Colonel Gabriel Yoryan, who formed the Council of the Salvation of the People. In 1983, Thomas Sankara became Prime Minister, but he was shortly thereafter imprisoned in Ouahigouya with Colonel Yoryan, Jean-Baptiste Ouedraogo, Blaise

Zongo, and Blaise Compoare. Blaise Compoare escaped. Returning with commandos three months later, he overthrew the regime and established the National Council of the Revolution with Sankara as President.

President Sankara struggled to reduce the suffering of his people. He established relations with other anti-imperialist governments such as Angola, Cuba, Ghana, Libya, and Zimbabwe. As a result, Burkina Faso's relations with more conservative countries, such as Côte d'Ivoire, Mali, France, and the U.S., deteriorated. Because Burkina Faso relies heavily on international aid, this was a difficult position to be in. On August 4, 1984, on the first anniversary of the revolution, Sankara renamed the impoverished Republic of Upper Volta "Burkina Faso." A combination of words from the Jula and More languages, Burkina Faso means the land of the upright people or the land of people with dignity.

In 1984 Sankara abolished the traditional tribute payments and obligatory labor for chiefs. He nationalized all the land and mineral rights. He abolished the taxation of rural citizens, canceled all rent for housing, reduced the high salaries of civil servants and military officers, began massive housing projects and vaccination programs, instituted compulsory military service, and held joint military maneuvers with Ghana.

In 1985 Sankara announced plans to plant

A Mossi teenager bathes in the rapids of the Black Volta River.

ten million trees to combat desertification and deforestation in northern Burkina Faso. In 1986 he launched the Alpha Commando literacy compaign. (Literacy is decreasing—by 1991, 80 percent of Burkinabe men and 91 percent of Burkinabe women were illiterate). That same year, 1986, he visited the Soviet Union, Cuba, Nicaragua, and Zimbabwe. In October 1987 he organized the Bambata Pan-African Anti-Apartheid Conference in Ouagadougou and passionately denounced apartheid. On October 15, 1987, Sankara was assassinated with twelve aides in a coup led by his trusted ally, Blaise Compoare.

Compoare, the new President, created the Popular Front and dissolved the National Council of the Revolution. Though he called upon the people to show their support for the coup, thousands of stunned and saddened Burkinabe filed past the makeshift graves over the next few days in silent protest. After several more years of political unrest, Compoare finally established a multiparty democracy with a constitution. However, his unpopular party remains in control.

Despite this turbulent history, Burkina Faso now has a constitution that enforces the separation of the government from the ruling political party. Most important, Burkina Faso has laws that prohibit torture and guarantee the protection of individual freedom.▲

# Glossary

**cash crops** Crops grown on plantations specifically for export.

**chattel slavery** Form of slavery practiced in the Americas whereby slaves were regarded as "things" belonging to their owners.

**desertification** The process whereby once fertile land becomes desert.

**direct rule** Rule of a colony directly by representatives of the colonizing group.

**domestic slavery** Form of slavery in which slaves were regarded as extensions of the family to which they were attached.

**ethnic** Cultural group.

**Imam** Religious leader in Islam.

**indirect rule** Rule of a colony through natives trusted by the colonizer.

*jihad* Muslim holy war.

**migrant laborer** Person who leaves his home to find paid work elsewhere.

**Mogho Naba** Title of a Mossi chief.

**Naba, Nab, Na** Titles for a Mossi king.

**polygamy** Customary law allowing one man to have two or more wives.

**revere** Hold in high esteem.

*yiri* House made of mud brick.

# For Further Reading

Afigbo, A.E.; Ayandele, E.A.; Gavin, R.J.;
Omer-Cooper, J.D.; Palmer, R. *The Making of
Modern Africa. The Twentieth Century. Volume 2.*
New York: Longman, 1986.

Barna, Joel Warren. "Gathering Force: T. Wheel-
er's Collection of Art from Burkina Faso."
*House and Garden.* v. 158:104, Apr. 1986.

Ellis, William S. "Africa's Sahel: The Stricken
Land." *National Geographic.* v. 172:140–79,
Aug. 1987.

Hammond, Peter B. *Yatenga: Technology in the
Culture of a West African Kingdom.* New York:
Free Press, 1966.

Harris, Joseph E. *Africans and Their History.* New
York: Penguin, 1987.

July, Robert W. *Precolonial Africa: An Economic
and Social History.* New York: Charles
Scribner's Sons, 1975.

Roy, Christopher D. *Art of the Upper Volta Rivers.*
Meudon: Chaffin, 1987.

———. "Mossi Zazaido." *African Arts.* v. 13(3):
42–47, 1980.

Skinner, Elliot P. *The Mossi of Burkina Faso:
Chiefs, Politicians, and Soldiers.* Prospect
Heights, IL: Waveland, 1992.

# Index

## ABOUT THE AUTHOR

Kibibi Voloria Mack-Williams received a BA in English from the University of Maryland at Eastern Shore in 1977 and an MA in African history from Northwestern University in 1982. She received a Ph.D. in the History of Women from the State University of New York in Binghamton in 1991 and is currently an Assistant Professor in the Black Studies Department at the University of Massachusetts, Boston. She has written several juvenile books on African and African-American people. She is currently completing a book on African-American women in South Carolina. Dr. Mack-Williams is the mother of four daughters.

## COMMISSIONING EDITOR
Chukwuma Azuonye, Ph.D.

## CONSULTING EDITOR
Gary van Wyk, Ph.D.

## PHOTO CREDITS
Christopher Roy, Ph.D.

## DESIGN
Kim Sonsky